BULLDOZERS

Amanda Askew

FIREFLY BOOKS

A FIREFLY BOOK

Published by Firefly Books Ltd. 2010

First printing

Publisher Cataloging-in-Publication Data (U.S.)
Askew, Amanda.
    Mighty machines : bulldozers / Amanda Askew.
[24] p. : col. photos. ; cm. (Mighty machines)
Includes index.
Summary: Includes bulldozers on building sites, bulldozers in mines and bulldozers in the army.
ISBN-13: 978-1-55407-703-8 (pbk.)
ISBN-10: 1-55407-703-6 (pbk.)
1. Excavating machinery -- Juvenile literature. 2. Bulldozers – Juvenile literature. I. Title.
[E] 624.1/52 dc22   TA735.A75 2010

Library and Archives Canada Cataloguing in Publication
Askew, Amanda
        Bulldozers / Amanda Askew.
(Mighty machines)
Includes index.
ISBN-13: 978-1-55407-703-8 (pbk.)
ISBN-10: 1-55407-703-6 (pbk.)
        1. Bulldozers--Juvenile literature. I. Title.
II. Series: Mighty machines (Richmond Hill, Ont.)
TA735.A85 2010   j629.225   C2010-901152-X

Published in the United States by
Firefly Books (U.S.) Inc.
P.O. Box 1338, Ellicott Station
Buffalo, New York 14205

Published in Canada by
Firefly Books Ltd.
66 Leek Crescent
Richmond Hill, Ontario L4B 1H1

Manufactured by 1010 Printing International Ltd. in Huizhou, Guangdong, China in May 2010, Job # JQ10010485.

Written by Amanda Askew
Designed by Phil and Traci Morash (Fineline Studios)
Editor Angela Royston
Picture Researcher Maria Joannou

Associate Publisher Zeta Davies
Editorial Director Jane Walker

Words in **bold** can be found in the Glossary on page 23.

Contents

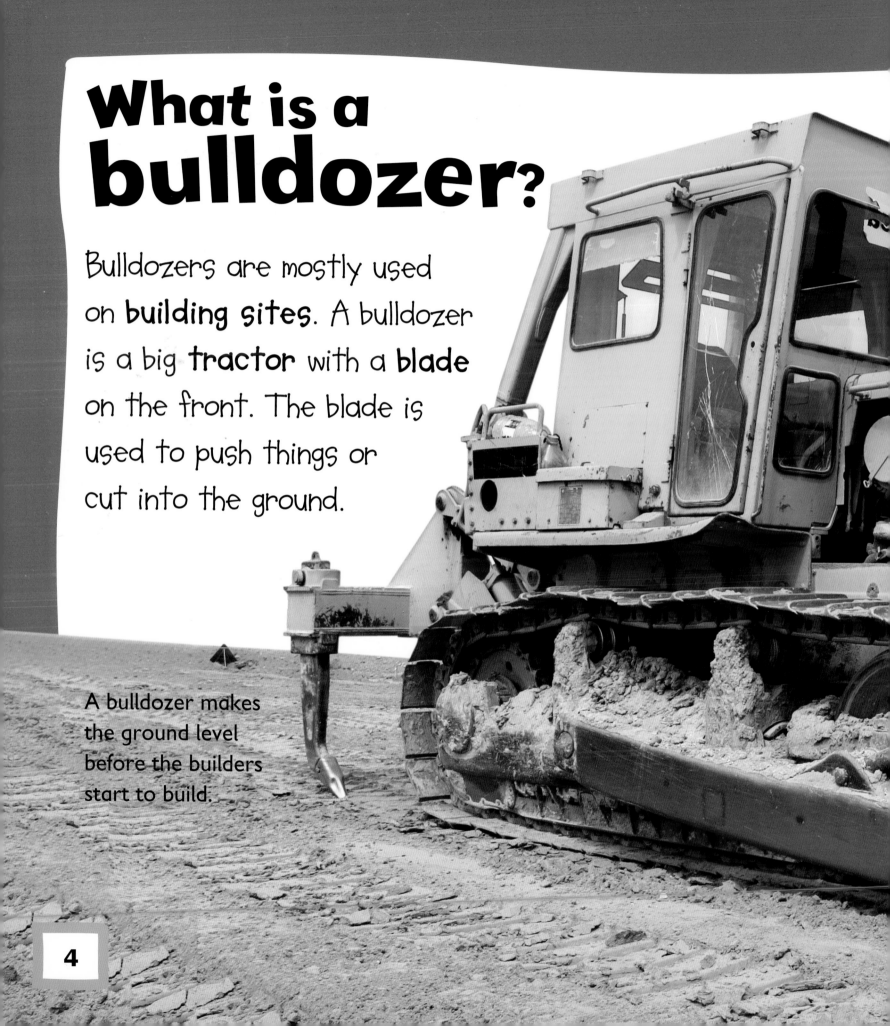

What is a bulldozer?

Bulldozers are mostly used on **building sites**. A bulldozer is a big **tractor** with a **blade** on the front. The blade is used to push things or cut into the ground.

A bulldozer makes the ground level before the builders start to build.

A bulldozer has **tracks** instead of wheels. The tracks help the machine to move across rough ground. If a bulldozer had wheels, it would probably slip and slide.

A bulldozer has wide tracks. They stop the machine from sinking into the ground.

Parts of a **bulldozer**

A bulldozer has two main parts — a tractor and a blade. When the blade pushes downwards, it cuts into the earth. When the blade pushes forwards, it moves the pile of earth.

tractor

The tractor is the main part of the bulldozer. The driver sits in the cab and controls the machine.

blade

cab

ripper

tracks

Blades and rippers

The bulldozer uses its blade to spread out uneven earth. This makes the ground flat.

The blade is on the front of the tractor. There are many shapes and sizes of blade. Most bulldozers have a straight blade, but some have curved blades.

The **ripper** is a large claw on the back of the tractor. The ripper "rips" into the ground and breaks it up.

This ripper is about to break up the hard ground.

Building roads

Tarmac has to be laid on flat ground. A bulldozer flattens the ground so a new road can be built.

The bulldozer pushes and spreads huge mounds of earth to make the road flat.

The bulldozer goes over the same ground many times. First, it spreads the large mounds of earth, and then it evens out any small lumps or bumps.

This bulldozer is making the ground even flatter.

11

Mining and quarrying

Large and small bulldozers are used at **mines** and **quarries**. They clear piles of rocks. The small machines can work where there isn't much room.

Some bulldozers use a special blade, called an "SU blade." The blade is so large, it can push piles of big rocks.

This SU blade turns up at the sides. The sides hold the rocks on the blade.

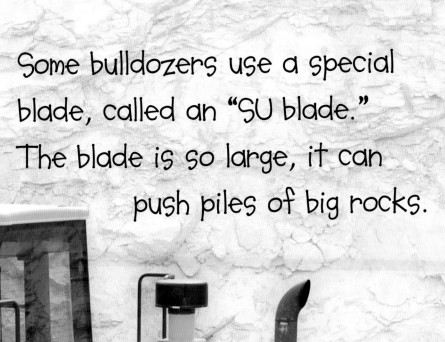

This machine is moving loose rocks.

In the army

Soldiers use bulldozers to clear a path through thick forests or across uneven land. Sometimes, a bulldozer blade is fitted to a tank.

These bulldozers and tanks are crossing rough ground.

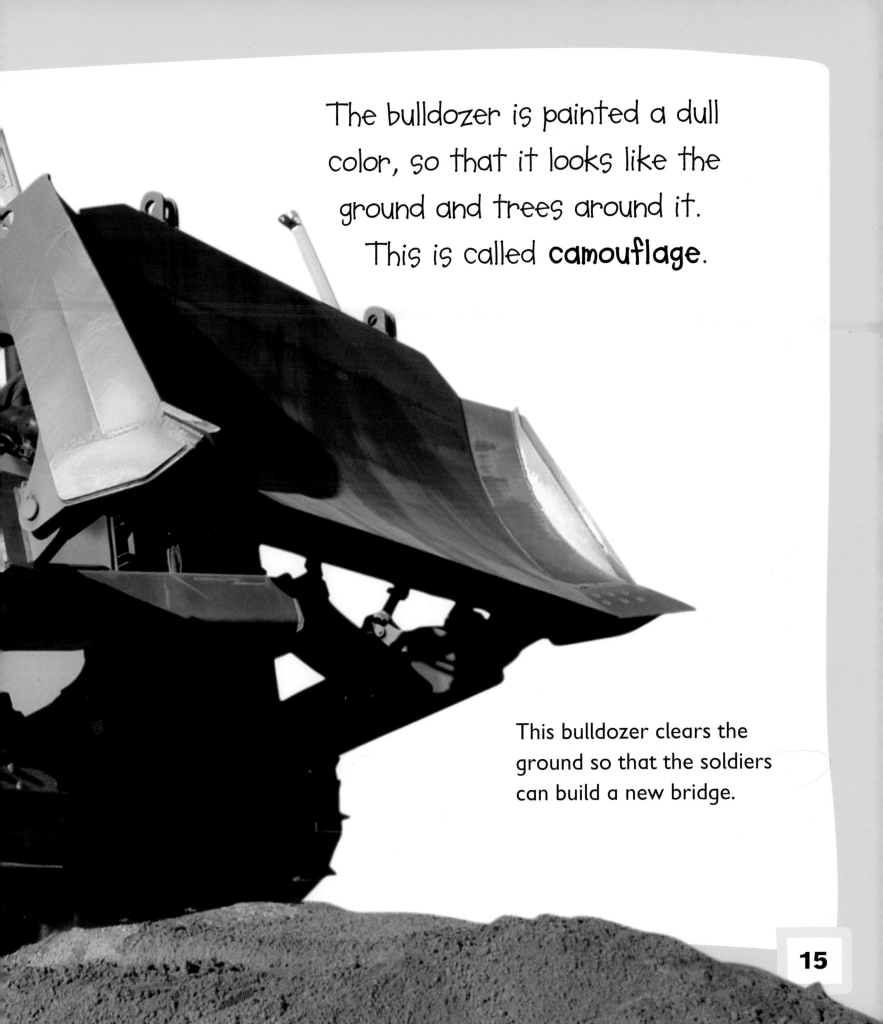

The bulldozer is painted a dull color, so that it looks like the ground and trees around it. This is called **camouflage**.

This bulldozer clears the ground so that the soldiers can build a new bridge.

On the farm

Some farmers use bulldozers to break up very hard ground. A **plow** cannot work when the ground is too hard.

The bulldozer is digging up the roots of a fallen tree.

A ripper is dragged through
hard ground to break it up.
The farmer can then plow the
land and plant crops.

A ripper can have
one spike or lots
of spikes.

Plowing the snow

Bulldozers make good **snowplows!** The blade clears a path through the snow or ice. The tracks stop the bulldozer from sliding on the slippery ground.

A snowplow stops cars and people from being blocked in by the snow.

A train can clear a track much faster than a bulldozer!

Trains can have a blade fitted to the front, just like a bulldozer. The blade clears snow from the railway tracks.

Biggest and smallest

The biggest bulldozer in the world is a Super Dozer. Its blade is 23 feet wide. Four adults could lie along it head to toe!

This monster machine can push 140 tons of rocks in one go. That's the same weight as 20 elephants!

KOMATSU

The blade on this mini bulldozer is less than 28 inches wide – no wider than two and a half of these books laid end to end!

Small machines are perfect for working in small spaces.

Activities

- Here are three bulldozers from the book. Can you remember what they do?

- If you needed to break up hard ground, which attachment would you use? Why did you choose that attachment?

- Draw a bulldozer building a road. Which bulldozer did you choose? What color is it? Who is driving it?

- Which picture shows a ripper?

Glossary

Blade
A large, flat attachment used for cutting or pushing earth.

Building site
A place where a house or other building is being built.

Camouflage
A way to hide something by making it the same color as the place it is in.

Mine
A deep hole in the ground. Coal is often found in a mine.

Plow
A machine that turns over the soil to make it ready for seeds to be planted.

Quarry
A place where stone and sand are dug out of the ground.

Ripper
An attachment with a spike or spikes for breaking up hard ground.

Snowplow
A machine that is used to move snow from roads.

Tarmac
A hard material used to make the surface of roads.

Tracks
A long, metal band around the wheels on a bulldozer.

Tractor
A farm machine with big wheels.

Index